ADV CHRISTMAS WITH THE CHURCH FATHERS

Marco Pappalardo

Libreria Editrice Vaticana

United States Conference of Catholic Bishops
Washington, D.C.

First printing, September 2010

ISBN 978-1-60137-115-7

CONTENTS

For my little niece

and for all of my friends' little children.

Through them

I have come to learn wonder;

through them

I have come to see daily life

from a new perspective;

through them

I have come to truly understand

what it means to be grown up.

INTRODUCTION

Holy Mother Church is conscious that she must celebrate the saving work of her divine Spouse by devoutly recalling it on certain days throughout the course of the year. Every week, on the day which she has called the Lord's day, she keeps the memory of His resurrection. In the supreme solemnity of Easter she also makes an annual commemoration of the resurrection, along with the Lord's blessed passion.

Within the cycle of a year, moreover, she unfolds the whole mystery of Christ, not only from His incarnation and birth until His ascension, but also as reflected in the day of Pentecost, and the expectation of blessed, hoped-for return of the Lord.

Recalling thus the mysteries of redemption, the Church opens to the faithful the riches of her Lord's powers and merits, so that these are in some way made present at all times, and the faithful are enabled to lay hold of them and become filled with saving grace.[1]

After the publication of my previous book, *Lent and Easter with the Church Fathers*, I would now like to humbly present the thoughts and meditations of some of the Church Fathers on the subjects of Advent and Christmas. Their writings constitute some of the most important documents in our history because of the richness of their content on multiple levels: spiritual, moral, dogmatic, and ascetic.

The Holy Father Benedict XVI began a series of Wednesday general audiences in March 2007 as a way of presenting the Fathers of the Church. The previous series was dedicated to the Apostles. This was a steady and profound catechesis in the full sense of the word, recounting the story of the Church through the lives of men who were important personalities during the first centuries of Christianity. Each time, attention was given to highlighting the originality, and at the same time the modern relevance, of each Church Father—some of whom are unknown to most people—so that he could instead become accessible to everyone.

The idea of this book, following the path set by the Holy Father's teachings, is to "draw out" the Church Fathers from the libraries or patristic archives in order to offer them to everyone, including those who are neither specialists, nor scholars, nor aficionados. Like its predecessor, this small book is not a text for study. It is intended to be a tool, even a daily companion, for personal and group meditation.

Anyone wishing to study these extraordinary men in greater depth can find works of great value, dense and impressive collections of their writings, monumental volumes, and monographic texts that are increasingly easy to access.

Each passage in this book is supplied with an introduction in italics by the editor, in order to provide a key to interpreting the selection and to bring the content to life for the modern reader.

Marco Pappalardo

Note
1   Second Vatican Council, *Sacrosanctum Concilium* (*Constitution on the Sacred Liturgy*), no. 102, in *The Documents of Vatican II*, ed. Walter M. Abbott (New York: Guild Press, 1966).

MEDITATIONS

First Week of Advent

Sunday

Maximus of Turin, *Homily 60*, 3-4

"The Mass has ended; go in peace!" How many times we have heard these words, and how often we instantly forget them as soon as we step foot outside the Church and meet with outstretched hands at the door, or once we have stopped at a red light. And yet the Mass just ended moments ago: we encountered Christ in the Eucharist! What does it mean to go in peace? What peace? Our heart should be restless after the celebration, ardently desiring consolation for those who suffer and striving to think of things to do for the poor, however great or small. The Mass does not end with the final blessing and recessional hymn; rather, this is the moment that it opens into our daily life.

Thus, dear brothers, may we who await the birth of the Lord cleanse ourselves of all the remnants of sin! Let us fill his treasuries with many gifts, so that upon the arrival of that holy day we may welcome the strangers, support the widows, and clothe the poor! Indeed, what would happen if, in the house of the servants under the same master, one were to proudly don silk garments while another was covered with rags; if one were stuffed with food while another suffered hunger and cold;

if one were tormented by indigestion from yesterday's gormandizing while another could hardly stave off yesterday's hunger? Or what should the purpose of our prayers be? May we who are not generous toward our brothers ask to be liberated from the enemy. Let us imitate our Lord! Indeed, if he desires that the poor partake of heavenly grace with us, why should they not partake of earthly goods with us? May those who are our brothers in the sacraments lack no earthly sustenance, even if only so they may give testimony before God on our behalf: may we sustain them and may they give thanks to him. The more a poor man blesses the Lord, the more it will help the one who gives him cause to bless the Lord.

MONDAY

Hilary of Poitiers, *Discourses*, I, 1ff.

In a world filled with uncertainty and doubt, where the only thing certain seems to be relativism, Christians find a clear reference point for salvation in Christ. In a faith perspective, waiting is not a waste of time: it does not mean sitting around idly, but rather being patient, which is a real, undeniable, and dynamic activity. Waiting is rejoicing in what truly matters even in the midst of difficulty; it is built on the rock and on what never withers; it is keeping silence, for it is in silence that we await Love and hear his footsteps.

O awaited one of the peoples! Those who await you will not be disappointed. Our fathers awaited you; all the righteous men from the beginning of the world have hoped in you and have not been confounded. Indeed, when your mercy was received in the heart of your temple, the joyful choruses made heard their praises and sang, "Blessed is he who comes in the name of the Lord!" (Mk 11:9). I have tirelessly awaited the Lord, and he has turned his gaze toward me. Then, recognizing divine majesty in the lowliness of flesh, they said, "Here is our God! We have awaited him; he will save us! He is the Lord; we have awaited him patiently, and we will exult and rejoice in his salvation!" . . . While others trouble themselves seeking their happiness down here, rushing to hoard the spoils, the world offers them without waiting for the fulfillment of the Lord's design. The blessed man who has placed his hope in the Lord and has not set his sights on vanity and deceptive folly keeps far from their ways. . . . And in thinking to himself, he consoles himself with these words: "My inheritance is the Lord, says my soul; that is why I will wait. The Lord is good to those who hope in him, to the soul that seeks him. It is good to wait in silence for God's salvation."

TUESDAY

John Chrysostom, *Homilies on the Gospel of Matthew*, 77, 2ff.

The soul is our true treasure and the greatest good we have. Without need for philosophical or theological reasoning, we all know full well—at least in theory—that we will bring nothing of real value with us to the grave except the way we have lived and made use of the talents we were given. All of this will not be buried with us, however, but will become a true treasure for heaven. We need to become cunning not so we can deceive our neighbor, but so we can avoid deceiving our soul for all eternity.

"Be sure of this: if the master of the house had known the hour of night when the thief was coming, he would have stayed awake and not let his house be broken into. So too, you also must be prepared, for at an hour you do not expect, the Son of Man will come" (Mt 24:43-44). He does not reveal the day, so that they will remain vigilant and ever ready; and he declares that he will come at the hour they least expect, so that they will remain constantly prepared for battle and dedicated to virtue. This is what his words ultimately mean: if men knew the time of their death, they would prepare for that hour in every way and with the greatest effort. That their fervor might not be limited to that day, he reveals neither the day of universal judgment nor the day of particular judgment; they will thus be always fervent and in constant expectation. This is the reason he leaves the end of every man's life in a veil of uncertainty. It seems to me that he also intends to rouse and confound the lazy, whose souls do not manifest the same concern as those whose riches instead lead them to fear the raids of a thief.

Wednesday

Eusebius of Caesarea, *Church History*, I, 2, 17ff.

The preannounced and long-awaited promise of the Old Testament is fulfilled at Christmas. The Messiah is God who becomes man for us. Everything in the Scriptures is a prelude to and preparation for this event that would become the heart of salvation history through his Death and Resurrection. It is the long-awaited occasion, our lover knocking at the door, and the reason we have made ourselves beautiful and dressed ourselves in festive attire. This divine time, this propitious moment, is not simply a memory today; rather, it is remembering and daily renewing God's offer of love for us.

This is the moment: behold, the Master of all virtues, the Father's Minister for the distribution all good things, the divine and heavenly Word, has appeared to all men, to all the peoples of the earth prepared and ready to receive the knowledge of the Father, through a man who is in no way different from our own nature in the essence of his body, and who has done and suffered what the prophets foretold. They had predicted that a God-Man, a worker of marvelous deeds, would come to the earth and become the Teacher of the Father's religion for all peoples; they had preannounced the wonder of his birth, the novelty of his teachings, the marvelousness of his works, and then the Death he would undergo, his Resurrection, and his divine return to the heavens. It is clear that all of this can be attributed to no one other than our Savior, the God-Word who was with God in the beginning and who, by his ultimate Incarnation, is also called the Son of Man.

THURSDAY

Caesarius of Arles, *Sermons*, 187, 3.5

"You see, my children, we cannot forget that we have a soul to save and an eternal life awaiting us. The world, wealth, pleasure, and honors will all pass; heaven and hell will never pass. Let us therefore be attentive!" These are the words used by the Holy Curé of Ars to address his faithful, and they invite each of us today to prepare a beautiful inner garment for the Lord and to seek out the best tailor—spiritual assistance—for the most fashionable event of our lives.

If the king of this world or a family father invited you to his birthday celebration, what garment would you wear other than the newest, most elegant, and most handsome one, so that neither its old age, nor little worth, nor any other unfavorable quality might be offensive in the eyes of your host? With equal care, then, as best you can and with the help of Christ, make sure you prepare your soul, adorned with the many ornaments of virtue, the jewels of simplicity, the flowers of temperance, a sure conscience, the beauty of chastity, the radiance of almsgiving, and the splendor of charity, for the solemn celebration of the Eternal King: the Nativity of Our Lord and Savior. Indeed, if Christ the Lord sees how well you have prepared yourself to celebrate his birth, he will deign not only to visit your soul, but also to rest and abide there forever, as it is written: "I will live with them and move among them" (2 Cor 6:16); and "behold, I stand at the door and knock. If anyone hears my voice and opens the door, [then] I will enter his house and dine with him, and he with me" (Rev 3:20).

Friday

Hilary of Poitiers, *Discourses*, I, 1ff.

Jesus was born two thousand years ago. This is a historical fact for everyone, and it is the starting point and destination of salvation history for those who believe. So what are we waiting for? We await the coming of Christ on the last day, which will be the beginning of the never-ending celebration. Yet the way we wait is also important. Here are some fitting words: gladness, hope, poverty in spirit, thoughts directed to God, and everlasting treasures. In this context Advent and Christmas are propitious moments for freeing the heart of anything that prevents us from aiming for the highest place and setting sail.

"We await the Savior." In truth, the righteous man's waiting is gladness, for he awaits the blessed hope and advent of the glory of our great God and Savior Jesus Christ. "What then am I awaiting," says the righteous man, "if not the Lord?" . . . Poor in spirit, be happy you have stored up your treasure in heaven in accordance with the advice of the heavenly Counselor, for fear that your heart, like your treasure, would come to know corruption if left on earth! Indeed, the Lord says, "For where your treasure is, there also will your heart be" (Mt 6:21). May your hearts therefore follow their treasure! Set your thoughts on heavenly things, and may your expectation hold fast to God, so that you may say as the Apostle says, "But our citizenship is in heaven, and from it we also await a savior, the Lord Jesus Christ" (Phil 3:20).

SATURDAY

Maximus of Turin, *Homily 60*, 3-4

How can we successfully convey the spiritual need for attention to the soul and not just the body in today's appearance-obsessed society? It's easy. The body will only last about one hundred years in a best-case scenario, but the soul lasts for all eternity. Who among us does not prepare as much as possible for an important event by cleaning up and putting on his or her nicest clothes? No one would want to look bad in front of others. We should prepare our soul in the same way, multiplied by eternity, so it will be clean and ready to participate in the feast of all feasts, the awarding of all awardings, the evening of all evenings, and the endless banquet, without making a poor impression on the other guests and particularly on the Lord of the house.

L et us therefore purify our heart, our conscience, and our spirit many days ahead of time, and thus cleansed and spotless let us prepare to receive the immaculate Lord who is coming. As he was born of the Immaculate Virgin, so too may his servants be immaculate to celebrate his birth! Indeed, anyone who is dirty and tainted on that day neither is concerned with the Nativity of Christ nor desires him. Such a man may well participate bodily in the feast of the Lord, but spiritually he is quite distant from the Savior; nor is it possible for an impure man and a holy man, an avaricious man and a merciful man, a corrupt man and a pure man to be together without the one offending the other, proving himself all the more unworthy the less he is aware of his unworthiness. Indeed, he causes insult though wishing to be courteous, like the man in the Gospel invited to the feast of the saints who dared to attend the wedding without a wedding garment (see Mt 22:1-14): while all the other guests radiated with justice, faith, and chastity, he alone—with an unclean conscience—was spurned by all the others for the repugnance he caused; and the more the sanctity of the holy guests shone, the more the insolence of his sins was revealed.

SECOND WEEK OF ADVENT

SUNDAY

Augustine, *Exposition on the Book of Psalms*, 33, 9

Praying is stretching a hand toward the Infinite. You are always heard. And no one ever really knows what he or she is asking. It is a loving dialogue between our own lowliness and the greatness of God. Our meager words, silence, abandonment, and meditation rise and go to the heavens. God will never hold back his hand when we turn to him with a sincere heart, with our limitations, and with our journey of faith. God does not simply grant us things; rather, he grants us what we most desire in the secrets of our heart that will bring us true happiness.

I sought the Lord and he answered me. Those who receive no answer are not seeking the Lord. Be attentive to your sanctity. The psalmist said neither "I have asked the Lord for gold and he has answered me," nor "I have asked the Lord for longevity and he has answered me," nor "I have asked the Lord for this and that and he has answered me." It is one thing to seek something from the Lord; it is another to seek the Lord himself. . . . Do not seek anything other than the Lord; but rather seek the

Lord himself, and he will answer you, and while you are still speaking he will tell you, "Behold, I am here." What does this mean? Behold, I am here: what do you wish, what would you like from me? Anything I could give you is nothing in comparison: take me, delight in me, and embrace me. Touch me with faith as soon as you can do so completely and I will unite with you, and I will free you from all your burdens so you can join with me fully: I will have transformed this mortal body of yours into immortality so you will be equal to my angels, you will always see my face, and you will be happy with no one to take you from your joy. For you sought the Lord and he answered you.

MONDAY

Hilary of Poitiers, *Commentary on Matthew*, 2, 2-4

John the Baptist's call to conversion resounds with the same power today that it did two thousand years ago. The desert of Judea is the emptiness of life, a lack of reference points, the loss of religious meaning, and decadence of values. God never abandons his people despite it all, and his Kingdom comes even closer through Christ's Resurrection. None of us is wholly pure and exempt from the need for repentance: those who believe they are risk hardness of heart and deafness to the call to change paths.

"In those days John the Baptist appeared, preaching in the desert of Judea [and] saying, 'Repent, for the kingdom of heaven is at hand!'" (Mt 3:1-2). The place could have been more suitable for the preacher, he might have had more comfortable garments and more suitable food; but given the facts it is an example of a performed action that is in itself a preparation. Indeed, he reaches the desert of Judea, which is a deserted region in terms of the presence of God, not of the people, and an empty region in terms of the abiding of the Holy Spirit, not of men: the place of his preaching bears witness to the abandonment of God by those to whom his preaching is directed. Since the Kingdom of Heaven is at hand, he launches an invitation to repentance through which one can turn away from error, abandon sin, and make a commitment to renounce all vice after being ashamed of it. He wants the deserted Judea to recall that it must receive him in whom the Kingdom of

Heaven is to be found in order to remain no longer empty in the future, on the condition that past vices be purified through the profession of repentance.

Tuesday

Fulgentius of Ruspe, *De Fide: To Peter*, 86

"Our entire religion is nothing but false religion, all our virtues are nothing but illusions, and we are merely hypocrites in the eyes of God if we do not have that universal charity toward all: the bad and the good, the rich and the poor, those who do wrong by us and those who do right by us. No, there is no virtue that better helps us understand that we are children of our great God than charity." These words of the Holy Curé of Ars remind us that everyone is given time to repent and it is not ours to judge, but rather to love.

Consider it extremely certain and do not doubt in the least that God's field is the Catholic Church, and within its fences the chaff is to be found among the wheat until the end of time. In other words, the good and the wicked are intermixed in the communion of the sacraments, and every office—priestly, religious, and lay— has both good and wicked men. Nor should the good be abandoned on account of the wicked; rather, on account of the good, the wicked must be tolerated to the extent required by faith and charity. . . . At the end of the world, it is certain that the good will be separated from the wicked even in body, when Christ will come with "his winnowing fan . . . in his hand to clear his threshing floor and to gather the wheat into his barn, but the chaff he will burn with unquenchable fire" (Lk 3:17). With righteous judgment he will separate the righteous from the unrighteous, the good from the wicked, the upright from the twisted, and he will place the good to his right and the wicked to his left, and, his mouth having pronounced the immutable sentence as just and eternal judge, the wicked will meet with eternal fire while the upright will find eternal life; the wicked will burn forever with the Devil while the just will reign forever with Christ.

WEDNESDAY

John Chrysostom, *Homilies on the Gospel of Matthew*, 36, 1-2

Jesus knows the secrets of our heart and shows himself to us in the ways we can recognize him. He knows that we often need tangible facts to touch with our own hands, but he calls blessed "those who have not seen and have believed" (Jn 20:29). Like the disciples of John the Baptist, we are moving toward Christ with our doubts, our fears, our weaknesses, our failings, and the little that we are, so he can fill us with his grandeur.

Indeed, the Gospel narrates that Jesus healed many of the sick after the arrival of the disciples of John [the Baptist]. What other conclusion could the messengers of John have drawn from this indirect response to their question? The Savior acts in this way because he knows full well that witness by deed is much more reliable and less suspect than witness by word. Essentially, being God and knowing full well the reason for which John had sent his disciples, Jesus Christ heals the blind, the lame, and others with infirmities not to show John his true nature—why should he demonstrate it to John, who already believed and obeyed him?—but only to instruct the followers of his forerunner who still nurtured doubts. This is why he told them, after having cured many of the sick, "Go and tell John what you have seen and heard: the blind regain their sight, the lame walk, lepers are cleansed, the deaf hear, the dead are raised, the poor have the good news proclaimed to them. And blessed is the one who takes no offense at me" (Lk 7:22-23). With these words, he clearly shows that he knows their most secret thoughts.

Thursday

Gregory the Great, *Homilies*, 6, 2-5

"I tell you, among those born of women, no one is greater than John; yet the least in the kingdom of God is greater than he" (Lk 7:28). Receiving such a compliment from Jesus must have been something extraordinary for John the Baptist, even though he did not receive it in person in this case. But this is much more than a gesture of affection: there is an awareness of the mission of the one who comes before, the need to prepare the way, and the expectation about to be fulfilled—an expectation that always involves an encounter. John's "not yet" transforms into Christ's "already." During Advent our expectation is therefore accompanied by the certainty of fulfillment: we know that the birth of the Lord will arrive after a precise number of days and weeks.

"Then why did you go out? To see a prophet? Yes, I tell you, and more than a prophet" (Mt 11:9). It is in fact the task of a prophet to predict the things of the future, not to indicate them. John is more than a prophet, because he indicates—by pointing him out—the one whose coming he foretold in his role as forerunner. But since he [John] is not a reed blowing in the wind, since he is not dressed in soft clothes, since the title of prophet is inadequate to describe his merits, let us therefore listen to learn how he may be fittingly called. [The Gospel] continues, saying that "this is the one about whom it is written: / 'Behold, I am sending my messenger ahead of you; / he will prepare your way before you'" (Mt 11:10). The Greek term used is the word for "angel," which is translated as "messenger." Rightly, therefore, the one who is sent to proclaim the High Judge is called an "angel," so that his title might reflect the dignity of the action he performs. It is certainly a noble title, but his life does not fall short of it.

FRIDAY

Augustine, *Exposition on the Book of Psalms*, 138, 16

Good and evil are not far removed from human experience: they are the light and darkness of everyday life. There is a human and material good that needs to be illuminated by the light of Christ to prevent it from becoming evil; there are adversities that can plunge us into the darkest of depths without the burning flame of faith. We can choose to follow the light of the star or to remain motionless, lamenting the darkness.

Thus it is night down here; but this night seems to have its light and its shadows. If we call it night in general, what is its light? The prosperity and happiness of this world, temporal joy, and temporal honors are the quasi-light of this night. But the adversity and bitterness of tribulations and dishonor are the shadows of this night. In this mortal life, in this night, men have both light and shadows: the light is prosperity and the shadows are adversity. But if Christ the Lord comes and inhabits the soul through faith, and promises it another light, and inspires it and grants it patience, and exhorts man not to take delight in prosperity and not to lose heart in adversity, then the faithful man begins to become different from this world, to not inflate himself when things go well and to not become disheartened when they go poorly, but to bless the Lord always and everywhere: not just when he has in abundance, but also when he has little; not just when he is healthy, but also when he is sick. Then the words of the psalm will be fulfilled in him: "I will bless the LORD at all times; / praise shall be always in my mouth" (Ps 34:2).

SATURDAY

Ephrem the Syrian, *Hymn for the Birth of Christ*, 1

What still astounds us is also what helps us to live each day with new eyes. On Christmas night in Bethlehem, many people must have experienced a wonder that rejuvenated them, drawing them outside of themselves and away from their concerns to follow the star, to seek a king, and to listen to the angels' song. What a special night that Christmas must have been! Now it is up to us to let ourselves still be amazed by the Father's grand gesture of love; it is up to us to believe in the Incarnation of the Son without a doubt, to be convinced of it, and to give witness to it by the strength of the Holy Spirit.

A man is overcome by great awe when he considers the miracle of God descending, abiding in a mother's womb, assuming a human body with his divine essence, willingly growing in his mother's uterus for nine months, and the fact that this womb made of flesh was able to carry such fire—a flame abiding in this delicate body without burning it. . . . The Virgin conceived God and the barren woman (Elizabeth) conceived the virgin (John); indeed, the child of barrenness sprouted before the shoot of virginity. God performed a new miracle among the inhabitants of the earth: he who "has marked off the heavens with a span" (Is 40:12) now lay in the tiny span of a manger; he who "has cupped in his hand the waters of the sea" (Is 40:12) was now born in a stable. The heavens are filled with his glory, and the manger was filled with his splendor. . . . Magnanimous is the wonder he has worked on our earth: the Lord of all has descended upon it, God has become man, the Ancient One has become a child, the Lord has made himself equal to his servants, and the Son of the King has made himself like a poor wanderer. The Most High has lowered himself and has been born into our nature, and he has assumed what was foreign to his own nature for our good. Who shall not joyfully contemplate the miracle of God lowering himself and submitting himself to birth? Who shall not be filled with awe in seeing that the Lord of the angels has been born? Believe it without doubting and be convinced that all of this has truly come to pass!

SOLEMNITY OF THE IMMACULATE CONCEPTION

DECEMBER 8

Ephrem the Syrian, *Hymns*, 18, 1

"Hail, bright Star of ocean, / God's own Mother blest, / ever sinless Virgin, / gate of heavenly rest; / Taking that sweet Ave, / which from Gabriel came, / peace confirm within us, / changing Eva's name. / Break the captive's fetters, / light on blindness pour, / all our ills expelling, / every bliss implore. / Show thyself a mother; / may the Word Divine, / born for us thine Infant, / hear our prayers through thine. / Virgin all excelling, / mildest of the mild, / freed from guilt, preserve us, / meek and undefiled; / Keep our life all spotless, / make our way secure, / till we find in Jesus / joy for evermore. / Through the highest Heaven / to the Almighty Three, / Father, Son, and Spirit, / one same glory be. Amen."[*] May it always be our custom and cause for rejoicing to praise the Immaculate Mary with hymns, songs, and prayers.

---

[*] Translation of *Ave, Maris Stella*, in *A Manual of Prayers for the Use of the Catholic Laity: Prepared and Published by the Third Plenary Council of Baltimore* (New York: Christian Press Association Publishing Company, 1896), 657-658.

Eve became guilty of sin and the debt was passed down to Mary, so that the daughter might pay the debts of the mother and lacerate the sentence that had transmitted her wailings to all generations. Mary carried flame in her hands and hugged the flame between her arms: she gave her breasts to the flame and her milk to him who nourishes all things. Who can speak of her? Earthly men multiplied the curses and thorns suffocating the earth and introduced death; the Son of Mary filled the world with life and peace. Earthly men introduced sickness and suffering and opened the door to death so that it might enter and walk about freely; the Son of Mary took the suffering of the world upon himself to save it. Mary is the most pure spring, untainted by tributaries: she welcomed into her womb the river of life, which irrigated the world with its waters and brought life to all the dead. . . . Two mothers appeared and generated different children: the one generated a man who cursed her, while Mary generated God, who fills the world with blessings.

Justin Martyr, *Dialogue with Trypho*, 99, 1-101

God always remains faithful to his covenant of love despite our weakness. He renews humanity with visible signs of mercy as part of his mysterious plan. Trusting in the angel's announcement, Mary the Virgin and Mother of God becomes both the instrument and protagonist of the action of divine grace. We too are called to be new men and women who are firm in faith, strong in witness, and steadfast in hope.

Ultimately, we understand that he became man of a virgin so that the disobedience that started with the serpent would be stopped through the very same path by which it began. Eve was a pure virgin: conceiving the word of the serpent, she gave birth to disobedience and death. The Virgin Mary instead conceived faith and joy when the angel Gabriel announced to her the good news that the Holy Spirit would descend upon her, that the power of the Most High would overshadow her, and that because of this the holy Being that would be born of her would be the Son of God. She responded, "May it be done to me according to your word" (Lk 1:38). She therefore gave birth to him whom the Scriptures mention so profusely, through whom God destroys the serpent—and the angels and men who are like the serpent—and delivers from death those who repent of their evil deeds and believe in him.

Cosmas the Singer, *Hymns*, 1899

The saints have a unique devotion to our Lady, and their thoughts fully express it. For example, take this quote of the Holy Curé of Ars: "The Most Blessed Virgin mediates between her Son and us. Despite the fact that we are sinners, she is filled with tenderness and compassion for us. Is not the child for whom the mother sheds the most tears the one closest to her heart? Does not a mother always take the greatest care of her weakest and most defenseless child?" Let us follow the path of the saints, enter the school of Mary, and welcome Jesus, who has come for our salvation.

Blessed Mother of God, open the door of your benevolence to us. May our trust, which rests in you, not be disappointed; deliver us from all adversity. You are the salvation of the human race. My sins are so many, O Mother of God! O Immaculate Mary, I have recourse to you in seeking salvation. Console my desolate soul and ask your Son, our Lord, to grant me forgiveness of my sins. O Immaculate One, blessed alone! I place all my hope in you, O Mother of Light: grant me your protection.

THIRD WEEK OF ADVENT

SUNDAY

Augustine, *Discourses*, 262, 4

Let us recognize the Son of God in the Child of Bethlehem. Let us recognize him just as he revealed himself to the world through the eyes of faith: the faith with which Mary received him into her womb, the elderly Simeon saw him, and the widow Anna honored him. Let us recognize Jesus, true God and true man, through the gospel accounts, the apostolic tradition, the teachings of the Church, and the words and lives of the saints.

Rise up, you who were closed within your mother's womb, you who formed yourself in she who was formed by you! You who were laid in the manger; you who suckled at the breast as an infant in the life of the flesh; you who carry the world and were carried by a mother; you whom the elderly Simeon acknowledged as little, yet glorified as great; you whom Anna the widow saw unweaned, yet proclaimed omnipotent; you who hungered for our sake; you who thirsted for our sake; you who grew tired along the road for our sake; you who did all of these things for our good; you who slept, yet did not fall asleep; you who in the end were sold by Judas, arrested, chained, scourged, crowned with thorns, fixed to the wood, and pierced by the lance after death; you who were killed and buried, rise above the heavens O God!

MONDAY

Origen, *Homilies on the Gospel of Luke*, 21, 2, 2-7

The proclamation of John the Baptist, fulfilled in the coming of Christ, reechoes throughout the time of Advent as an uninterrupted voice traveling from nation to nation and heart to heart. Hearing alone is insufficient to accept the invitation to prepare the way of the Lord; rather, an inner listening is necessary for the invitation to be effective in our lives and in the lives of others. Let us make time each day for an encounter with Christ so he will not run into the obstacles of boredom, sadness, sin, anxiety, superficiality, possessiveness, and greed.

We find this passage from the Old Testament in the Book of the Prophet Isaiah: "A voice cries out: / In the desert prepare the way of the LORD! / Make straight in the wasteland a highway for our God!" (Is 40:3). The Lord seeks to find in you a pathway to enter your soul and complete his journey; thus, prepare for him that path of which it has been written to "make straight in the wasteland a highway." "A voice cries out": there is thus a voice calling to "prepare the way." Indeed, the voice is first to reach the ears; then, after the voice, or rather together with the voice, comes the word that penetrates the hearing. It is in this sense that John proclaimed the Christ. Thus, let us see what the voice proclaims with regard to words. It says to "prepare the way of the LORD." What way should we prepare for the Lord? Is it a physical pathway? Can the word of God follow such a pathway? Or is it perhaps necessary to prepare instead an inner pathway for the Lord, setting up straight and level paths into our hearts? It is through this type of path that the Word of God enters, taking up his place in the human heart that is ready to welcome him.

TUESDAY

Basil the Great, *Exhortation to Baptism*, 7-8

"How sad, my children! Most Christians do nothing other than work to satisfy this 'corpse' that will soon decay in the earth, with no regard for their poor souls destined for happiness or unhappiness in all eternity. Their lack of spirit and good sense is chilling!" These words of the Holy Curé of Ars are truly powerful and bear all the suffering of a spiritual father and a tireless confessor. How wonderful it would be to reread them with a converted heart, replacing its key words with their opposites: "joyful," "achieve the eternal fate of happiness we build while on this earth," "commitment to the soul," "lively and hopeful spirit," and "serene and inspired minds."

Learn from the [gospel] example of the virgins. Indeed, having no oil left in their lamps, yet needing to enter the wedding feast of the bridegroom, they realized that they lacked what was indispensible when it was already too late. . . . You, too, must be on guard: if you wait year after year, month after month, and day after day to procure oil for the lamp, then in the end, as you feel your life begin to fade, you will suddenly feel nothing but suffering and affliction with no remedy. . . . Do everything possible to make yourself worthy of the Kingdom. Do not disdain the invitation you have received. Do not offer excuses, availing yourself of one pretext or another. I am unable to hold back the tears when I think to myself about the fact that, when you choose shameful works rather than the radiant glory of God and embrace sin without hesitation, you exclude yourself from the promised goods and prevent yourself from contemplating the goods of the heavenly Jerusalem. It is here where the infinite hosts of angels, the multitudes of firstborn sons, the thrones of the Apostles, and the seats of the prophets are found; it is where the scepters of the patriarchs and the crowns of the martyrs are admired and where the praises of the just are sung. After you have been purified and sanctified by the gifts of Christ, stir up in yourself the desire to be counted among all of these as well.

WEDNESDAY

Clement of Rome, *Second Letter to the Corinthians*, 8-9

There is no time other than this life for the fulfillment of God's dream of happiness for us. We are free to choose the path of life or the path of death, not just physically, but above all spiritually. Both dimensions are connected and will be condemned or sanctified together, just as salvation has been granted us through Jesus, who became man, died, and rose from the dead for us. The path of life is not required, but the trail has been blazed, and it's up to us to follow the signals and directions.

L et us do penance so long as we are still on this earth, dear brothers, for we are like clay in the hands of the potter. So long as the pot breaks or becomes misshapen while the potter is still molding it, he can set his hand to it once more; but otherwise, if he has already put it in the oven, there is no longer anything he can do about it. We too, dear brothers, can repent with all our heart of our sins committed in the flesh so long as we remain on this earth, thereby obtaining salvation from the Lord while we are still in time; once we have left this world, however, we will no longer be able to do penance and confess our sins. Thus, dear brothers, we will gain eternal life only if we comply with the will of the Father, keeping our bodies pure and fulfilling the commandments of the Lord. Indeed, he warns us in the Gospel with these words: "The person who is trustworthy in very small matters is also trustworthy in great ones; and the person who is dishonest in very small matters is also dishonest in great ones. If, therefore, you are not trustworthy with dishonest wealth, who will trust you with true wealth?" (Lk 16:10-11). . . . You have been called in the flesh: thus, you will reach God in the flesh. If Christ, our Lord and Savior, was only spirit in the beginning and then took flesh and called us in this way alone, then it is only in this flesh of ours that we too will gain our eternal reward.

Thursday

Augustine, *Tractates on the Gospel of St. John*, 4, 1

A true friend is ready to do anything for his or her friend. The greatest gift that can be given in a friendship is making way for the other by taking a step back at the right time. John the Baptist, described as a solitary man of the desert, fully understood this relationship and how a spiritual bond cannot be neglected. He stepped back at the appropriate time, indicating the true Teacher for his disciples; however, he did not step back from the presence of this quintessential Friend— the Bridegroom—at the time of the Baptism in the Jordan. From that moment on, he remained his witness to the point of martyrdom.

You have often heard it said, and are thus perfectly aware, that the more John the Baptist stood out among all those born of woman and the more he humbled himself before the Lord, the more he deserved to be a friend of the Bridegroom. He was filled with zeal for the Bridegroom, not for himself; he sought not his own glory but that of his judge, whom he preceded as a herald. Thus, while the ancient prophets had the privilege of preannouncing the future events regarding the Christ, John had the privilege of directly identifying him. Indeed, just as Christ was not recognized by those who did not believe the prophets before his coming, so he was not recognized by those among whom he was present once he came. For he came humbly and quietly at first: the more humbly, the more quietly. But the people, disdaining the humility of God through their pride, crucified their savior and thereby made him their judge.

Friday

Origen, *Homilies on the Gospel of Luke*, 21, 2, 2-7

In the age of GPS navigators, let's keep in mind who is guiding our lives, where our actions are directed, and which roads we need to take to reach our final goal. No technology can replace our conscience, but there are many ways to disorient and distract it. During this time of expectation, let's learn to synchronize our consciences with true values, with courageous though unpopular decisions, and with actions for the common good and not just personal profit: let's synchronize ourselves to God's wavelength.

In order to bring simple men to recognize the greatness of the human heart, I will offer a few examples from daily life. As numerous as the cities we have visited may be, we keep them all in our spirit: their qualities, the locations of their squares, the positions of their walls, and their buildings remain in our heart. We remember the road we have traveled, which is drawn and etched upon our memory. In our silent thoughts, we carry the sea that we have crossed. As I have told you, the human heart cannot be small if it is able to contain much. And if it is not small, since it contains many things, then one can very well prepare the way of the Lord, blazing a straight path so that the Word and Wisdom of God may enter. Prepare a road for the Lord by honest conduct, level the paths with worthy works, so that the Word of God may walk within you without finding obstacles and may give you knowledge of his mysteries and his coming: he "to whom belong glory and dominion forever and ever" (1 Pt 4:11).

SATURDAY

John Chrysostom, *Homilies on the Gospel of Matthew*, 20, 5ff.

If someone showed us a safe place to keep our treasure on this earth, we would not hesitate to follow him or her even if it was out of the way, and we would place our treasure there with great peace of mind. Well, it is no human being but God himself who offers this safety, and not in a desert, but in heaven; yet we do not want to listen to him. Our Author is inviting us to listen to the Word of God and follow it, to invest in the bank of heaven, where tax-free interest is always accruing for us.

Even if your goods were completely safe here on earth, you would not cease to be restless and uneasy. Indeed, you might not lose your riches, but you certainly would not be able to free yourself of the concern and fear of losing them. But once they are guarded above, you will have nothing to fear. Not only will your gold be perfectly safe, but it will bear fruits. Your money will thus become both treasure and seed at the same time. In fact, it will be something even more. Seed does not last forever, but your gold, thus multiplied, will last eternally. The treasure you bury here below neither blossoms nor bears fruit; on the other hand, if you deposit it in heaven, it produces fruits that will never decay. . . . Thus, so long as we still have some time left, we should use our faculty of speech to ask for graces both early and often: we need to obtain abundant oil and store it in heaven. If we do so, then through the grace and mercy of our Lord Jesus Christ we will find and enjoy all these goods at the proper time and when we have great need of them.

Fourth Week of Advent

Sunday

Hilary of Poitiers, *On the Trinity*, 2, 24-25

"I, Joseph, was walking yet stopped walking. I looked up in the air and saw it was struck with wonder; I looked toward the vault of the sky and saw it was still, and the birds of the sky were still; I looked at the earth and saw a trough on the ground and workers reclining with their hands in it, but those who were chewing stopped chewing, those who were getting their food did not lift it from the trough, and those who were bringing it to their mouths halted; all eyes were looking above. There were sheep that had been prodded forward yet were standing still; the shepherd lifted his hand to strike them, but his hand held still in the air. I saw the current of the river and the goats' mouths resting upon the water, but they were not drinking. Then, in an instant, everything continued its course" (Protoevangelium of James, 18). As this passage from one of the apocryphal gospels recounts, all creation stood still for an instant when Christ was born. We too should be still, in awe, in order to contemplate the beauty of this immense gift.

T he Son of God was born of the Virgin and the Holy Spirit for the human race, becoming his own servant in this work. . . . In this manner, having become man through the Virgin, he took upon himself the nature of the flesh so that the body of the entire human race might be sanctified through this intimate union. . . . What could we ever repay him that might be worthy of such love and condescension? The firstborn of God, one with God in his ineffable origin, enters the womb of the Blessed Virgin to grow as a human fetus. He who contains all, in whom and for whom all things are, comes into the world like every other man. He whose voice makes the angels and archangels tremble and melts the skies and the earth and all the elements of this world makes heard his infant wailing. He who is invisible and incomprehensible, who cannot be measured by sight, sense, or touch, is laid down with care in a manger. If anyone considers this beneath God, he thereby acknowledges himself as the recipient of a good so much the greater. . . . He had no need to become man: man was already made through him. It was we who needed God to become man and dwell among us.

MONDAY

Augustine, *Discourses*, 189, 3

Mary's "yes" is the unique measure of all our "yeses" to the Lord. Her adherence to God's plan becomes the model for our participation in the divine plan for this world. Mary was the "daughter of his Son," as Dante calls her, and we will be reborn as children and renewed in his mercy if we live our daily lives in praise of the Most High and in service to our brothers and sisters.

Christ the Lord exists eternally without beginning with the Father, and yet today you can ask, "What is it?" It is the Nativity. "Whose?" The Lord's. "So the Lord has been born?" Yes. "The Word who was in the beginning, God with God, has thus been born?" Yes. If he had not been born as a human being, we would never have attained divine rebirth. He was born so that we might be reborn. Christ is born: may no one hesitate to be reborn! He was generated, but not to be regenerated. . . . This is how his mercy was infused into our hearts. The Virgin became gravid with the Incarnation of the Son: may our hearts be gravid with faith in Christ! The Virgin gave birth to the Savior: may our souls give birth to salvation and may we give birth to praise! Let us not remain barren: may our souls be fertile for God!

Tuesday

Ambrose, *Concerning Virginity*, II, 2, 7

Mary, the Mother of God, is present during all the crucial moments of the life of her Son and of the nascent Church. She doesn't speak many words, but each one has great weight in the economy of salvation. St. Ambrose tells us about Mary in her daily life, speaking about her with wisdom from on high, presenting her as a lofty yet attainable model of virtue for each of us. Every once in a while, maybe we should adopt one of Our Lady's attitudes while praying the Rosary so that our prayer will become efficacious in our lives and not remain mere words.

The magnanimity of the teacher is the first thing that excites enthusiasm for learning. Now, who could be more magnanimous than the Mother of God? Who could be more splendid than she who generated the Body of Christ without tainting her own? And, truly, what is left to say about the other virtues? She was a virgin not just in her body but in her soul: she never stained the transparency of her spirit with any dark aspirations. She was humble of heart, austere of words, prudent of spirit, measured of speech, yet very eager to learn. She set her hope not upon the uncertain possession of riches but upon the prayers of the poor. Purposeful in her work and modest in her listening, she wanted not man but God as the only judge of her soul; she did not contradict anyone, had goodwill toward everyone, recognized the authority of elders, was not jealous of her peers, shunned vainglory, followed good sense, and loved virtue.

Wednesday

Athanasius, *Defense Against the Arians*, III, 31

What is closer to us than the flesh, which covers and swathes us like a cloak? What is more concrete than the flesh from which we are born and which will abandon us when we die? What is more human than the flesh that brings us into contact with others and allows us to procreate, suffer, and rejoice? We should not fear the flesh and our humanness, but we are called to avoid enslavement to them. The God-Christ took upon himself what was most human in order to make it divine: he did not take a body from someone else; on the contrary, the body he offered up on the Cross was his own.

The Word was born of Mary to destroy sin (indeed, the Father thought well to send his Son born of woman and subject to the law), hence it is said that he took flesh and became man. And while in this flesh, he suffered for us: as Peter says, "Christ suffered in the flesh" (1 Pt 4:1). This was so that it would be clear and all would believe that he who was always God sanctified those with whom he came to abide, ordered all things according to the will of the Father, became man for us, and as the Apostle says, "in him dwells the whole fullness of the deity bodily" (Col 2:9). Thus, the Word bore the infirmities of his flesh, because the flesh was his. And the flesh, in turn, served as an instrument of divine works, for the deity was in the flesh, and the flesh was the body of God.

Thursday

Ambrose, *Concerning Virginity*, II, 2, 12-13

Mary teaches us wisdom, substance, service, patience, hope, courage, humility, trust, and charity. Her heart is a jewelry box safeguarding these gifts and many others. It was unlocked for us at the foot of the Cross, which was its key. In a society of noise, gossip, and empty words, we are called to think and make concrete decisions with discretion, sobriety, and, most importantly, meditative silence.

The moment Mary learned she was chosen by God, she became even more humble and immediately set out on a journey toward the mountains to visit her relative; this was certainly not because her faith needed a confirmation, for she had already assented to the divine annunciation. Indeed, she heard these words [from her cousin]: "Blessed are you who believed" (Lk 1:45). Then she remained with her for three months. In such a long period of time, she did not seek to find evidence for her faith, but gave evidence of her charity. And all of this after the infant, exulting in his mother's womb, had greeted the mother of the Lord. . . . Later, when all of those wonders—a barren woman giving birth, a virgin woman conceiving a child, a mute man speaking, the Wise Men's adoration, Simeon's waiting, the guidance of the star—were accomplished, Mary remained imperturbable despite having been frightened by the angel's arrival, and, as it is written, she "kept all these things, reflecting on them in her heart" (Lk 2:19).

FRIDAY

Athanasius, *Defense Against the Arians*, III, 29-30

This selection is taken from a work that was written in defense of the faith at a time when the Church was suffering at the hand of heresies, teachings that deviate from the original gospel message and apostolic Tradition. This reading may seem somewhat complicated, but it helps us delve more deeply into the mystery of the Incarnation of Christ. It points out where to look in the Bible for all the content of our faith, which cannot be reduced to a children's story but, by the same token, should not be subject to sophistication and debates about chief world systems.

The purpose and nature of the Holy Scriptures, as I have oftentimes repeated, is the proclamation of a twofold doctrine regarding the Savior: he is and has always been God and Son, being the Word and Splendor and Wisdom of the Father; and, later on, having taken flesh for us through Mary, the Virgin Mother of God, he became man. May he who reads the Scripture learn the words about the Word in the Old Testament, and observe the Lord made man in the Gospel. Indeed, the Gospel tells us that "the Word became flesh / and made his dwelling among us" (Jn 1:14). He did not come in a man, but rather became man. . . . If he had simply appeared in a man, there would have been nothing wondrous about it. . . . Instead, now that the Word of God, through whom all things were made, did not refuse to become the Son of Man and humble himself by taking the form of a slave, Christ crucified is "a stumbling block to Jews and foolishness to Gentiles, but to those who are called . . . Christ the power of God and the wisdom of God" (1 Cor 1:23-24). "The Word," John says, "became flesh" (Jn 1:14).

SATURDAY

Rufinus of Aquileia, *Commentary on the Apostles' Creed*, 8-9

In the writings of the Holy Curé of Ars, we read that "when we talk about earthly matters, such as business and politics, we quickly grow tired; but when we talk about the Blessed Virgin, it is as though the matter were ever new. All the saints were strongly devoted to the Blessed Virgin, and no grace comes from heaven without first passing through her hands. One cannot enter a house without speaking first with the porter: well then, the Blessed Virgin is the porter of heaven!" The following excerpt arose in a much different context than the one just cited, was intended for a different audience, and uses a different tone and style—but we never grow tired of praising the Immaculate Virgin Mary and Mother of God.

Indeed, the world has now been given a new birth, and not without reason. Indeed, he who is the unique Son in heaven is therefore also unique on earth and is born in a unique way. Regarding this point, the words of the prophets in the Gospels are reechoed and well known: "The virgin shall be with child, and bear a son" (Is 7:14; see Mt 1:23; Lk 1:31). The prophet Ezekiel had already indicated birth as the marvelous mode of his arrival, symbolically defining Mary as the Gate of the Lord: he entered the world through this gate. . . . He came through this gate, from the Virgin's womb, and the gate of the Virgin remained eternally sealed because her virginity was preserved. For this reason, the Holy Spirit is called the creator of the Lord's flesh and of its temple.

SOLEMNITY OF
CHRISTMAS

DECEMBER 25

Gregory of Nazianzus, *Oration 38*, 1

May our bodies be living crèches every day and everywhere we are called to live as true Christians. May our legs, step by step, be like those of the animals that visited the grotto in Bethlehem so all creation could praise its Creator. May our bellies be like Mary's when she accepted Christ and allowed him to grow within her; we can continue accepting him in the Eucharist. May our arms be like Joseph's when they cradled, lifted, hugged, and served Jesus; we can do the same daily by embracing our brother and sisters, working, studying, and serving. May our mouths and voices be like those of the angels, that we may always sing and give praise in a loud voice to the Word made flesh: "Glory to God in the highest" (Lk 2:14). May our ears and eyes be like those of the shepherds, who heard the angels' song wherever they were and came to see the Child. May our intellect be like that of the Magi, who saw the star, had faith, and set off on their journey: an intellect that allows itself to be struck with wonder by a Child who is the Son of God, by the God who became like us so that we might become like him. May our hearts be like the manger that held the Eternal One, who became so little to turn our poverty into true wealth and joy. Amen.

Christ is born: sing glory! Christ has descended from heaven: go out to meet him! Christ is on earth: lift yourselves up! "Sing to the LORD, all the earth" (1 Chr 16:23), for he who belongs to heaven is now on earth! Christ has become flesh, so tremble and rejoice: tremble because of sin and rejoice because of hope! Christ is born of the Virgin. . . . Who does not adore him who is the beginning? Who does not praise and glorify him who is the end? The darkness is once more dispelled, the light is once more created, Egypt is once more tormented by the darkness, and light is once more shed upon Israel by the pillar of fire. May the people who are in the darkness of ignorance see the magnificent light of knowledge. "The old things have passed away; behold, new things have come" (2 Cor 5:17).

Gregory the Great, *Homilies*, 1, 8

The meaning of Christmas, the central event of salvation history and the prelude to the Resurrection, is relived today in the hearts of men and women of goodwill. They will never tire of proclaiming, by their prayers and their lives, "Glory to God in the highest / and on earth peace to those on whom his favor rests" (Lk 2:14). They never lose sight of heavenly things, especially the divine encounter with Christ in the Eucharist as true food and drink: this feast is not limited to just Christmas Day and Easter Sunday.

What does this worldwide census upon the day of the Lord's birth mean, if not that he who has written his elect in the book of eternity is entering the world in the flesh? The prophet says of the wicked, "Strike them from the book of the living; / do not count them among the just!" (Ps 69:29). And the Lord was rightly born in Bethlehem, for Bethlehem means "house of bread." Indeed, he is the one who says, "I am the living bread that came down from heaven" (Jn 6:51). The place where the Lord was born was thus known even before his birth as the "house of bread," for he who would satisfy the elect with spiritual nourishment would manifest himself there. And he was not born in a house, but rather along the road, to show that by taking on human nature he was born into a role that was not his own. It was not his own, we say, because as God his proper nature is divine. Yet the human nature belonged to him because God is the master of all, and therefore it is written that "he came to what was his own" (Jn 1:11).

Jerome, *Homily on the Nativity of the Lord*, 31-40

Nowadays it is increasingly apparent how the meaning of Christmas is becoming lost. Everything is focused on buying and selling gifts. The tree replaces the crèche, Santa Claus replaces Baby Jesus, hurriedness overtakes meditation, and noise wins out over listening. Our society has forgotten the true guest of honor and the whole reason for Christmas. That's like everyone coming to our birthday party with presents for a relative or friend instead of for us. Yet there would be no crèches, trees, lights, Santa Claus, eggnog, celebrations, or presents if Jesus had not become human two thousand years ago in order to make us like him. This does not mean we should not celebrate, rejoice, play, eat, and exchange gifts: the question is simply, For whom should we be doing it?

O h, if only I could see that manger in which the Lord was laid! As a tribute of honor, we Christians have now removed the mud-baked one and replaced it with a silver one; but the one that has been removed is more precious to me! Silver and gold are appropriate for the pagan world: the manger of baked mud is more fitting for the Christian faith. He who was born in this manger disdains gold and silver. I do not disapprove of those who do it to honor him (nor, in truth, do I disapprove of those who made golden vases for the temple); rather, I am amazed that the Lord and Creator of the world was not born amid gold and silver, but in the mud.

Romanos the Melodist, *Hymns*, 10, Prelude 1, 2

Who knows how intensely Mary gazed upon her little Jesus? Who knows how moving Mary's kisses, caresses, and embraces were for her little Jesus? Who knows how sweet his crying and laughing were for Mary? We do know, however, that one day we will enjoy all of this, for the prophet Isaiah says that "a child is born to us, a son is given us; / upon his shoulder dominion rests" (Is 9:5).

B ethlehem has reopened Eden, and we will see how. We have found its delights in a hidden place, and in the grotto we will regain the goods of Paradise. The root has appeared there, watered by no one, and from it forgiveness has blossomed. The well has been found there, dug by no one, from which David once sought to drink. By giving birth there, a virgin instantly quenched the thirst of Adam and the thirst of David. Therefore let us hurry to this place where the God who is, before all time, has been born as a little child. The Mother's Father, by his own free choice, has become her child; the savior of newborns is a newborn himself, lying in a manger. His mother meditates upon him and says to him, "Tell me, my child, how were you planted within me; how were you formed? I see you with awe, O flesh of mine, for my bosom is filled with milk but I have had no spouse; I see you wrapped in swaddling clothes, and yet the seal of my virginity remains intact. Indeed, it is you who have preserved it while deigning to come into the world, my child, you who are God before all time."

FEAST OF
ST. STEPHEN

DECEMBER 26

Fulgentius of Ruspe, *Sermons for the Feast of St. Stephen*, 1, 3-6

Fulgentius creates a poetic parallel between the persons of Jesus Christ and Stephen. Today we see the wonders of both Christmas and Easter, which together made Stephen an imitator of Christ. He contemplates the glory of the risen Christ, proclaims his divinity, entrusts his spirit to him, forgives his murderers, and delights in the presence of the Father.

Yesterday we celebrated our eternal King's birth into time; today we celebrate the triumphant passion of the soldier. Indeed, yesterday our King deigned to visit the world, bearing our flesh, by coming forth from the womb of the Virgin; today the soldier, coming forth from the tent of his body, has entered triumphantly into heaven. The former, while preserving the majesty of his eternal divinity, descended to fight on the battlefield of the world; the latter, stripped of the corruptible garment of the body, ascended to the heavenly palace to reign in eternity. The former descended bearing the flesh, while the latter ascended crowned with martyrdom. The latter ascended, stoned by the Jews, because the former had descended amid the jubilation of the angels. Yesterday the holy angels sang, "Glory to God in the highest" (Lk 2:14); today they welcomed Stephen into their ranks. Yesterday the Lord came forth from the womb of the Virgin; today the soldier came forth from the prison of the flesh. Yesterday Christ was wrapped in swaddling clothes for us; today Stephen was clothed by him with the stole of immortality. Yesterday the narrow space of a manger welcomed Christ the Child; today the immensity of heaven triumphantly welcomed Stephen.

Augustine, *Sermons*, 315, 7

"Whoever believes in me will do the works that I do, and will do greater ones than these" (Jn 14:12). These were the words of Jesus to his disciples. Stephen understood them well and put them into practice, just as his teacher had done on the Cross by forgiving his persecutors in his final moment of life. This is the imitation of Christ! And what about us? A little bit of important advice comes to us from the Holy Curé of Ars: "When the Devil stirs up feelings of hatred within us toward those who have hurt us, the only way to catch him offguard is to pray for them immediately. This is how you can defeat evil with good, and this is what it means to be holy."

Christ teaches the rules of mercy from the podium of the Cross. He has Stephen as a disciple who imitates him. What Stephen was in his humility, Christ was in a sublime manner; what Stephen did while turned to the ground, Christ effectuated while hung to the Cross. Indeed, recall that it was Christ himself who said, "Father, forgive them, they know not what they do" (Lk 23:34). He stood up at the podium of the Cross and taught the rules of mercy. O Good Teacher, you spoke well and you taught us rightly. Here is your disciple who prays for your enemies and prays for his murderers. The humble disciple has taught us how to imitate the sublime Teacher, the creature how to imitate the Creator; the victim how to imitate the Mediator, the man how to imitate the God-Man! . . . The God-Christ, as a man upon the Cross, taught us unquestionably when he said in a clear voice, "Father, forgive them, they know not what they do" (Lk 23:34).

FEAST OF THE HOLY INNOCENTS

DECEMBER 28

Leo the Great, *Sermon 33, 4*

The children and little ones will go before us into the Kingdom of Heaven. The Holy Innocents are unknowing martyrs immediately associated with Christ's sacrifice on the Cross and the glory of the Resurrection, because there is merely a temporal gap—not a spiritual one—between Christmas and Easter. This occasion helps us to "become like children" (Mt 18:3). May it encourage us to fight for life from the moment of conception and urge us to defend the little children of the world. Tears and occasional donations are not enough: we are called to real action.

After having worshiped the Lord and completed their devotion, the Wise Men follow the warning they received in a dream and return home by a different route. Indeed, having faith by now in Christ, it was necessary that they cease traveling the paths of their old lives: having taken up a new path, they were to leave their errors behind. Furthermore, they did not return by the old path in order to thwart the snares of Herod, who had deceptively prepared a cruel plot against the Child Jesus. His hopeful plan thus falling to ruin, the flames of the king's rage were fanned with fury. Remembering the time frame indicated by the Wise Men, he unleashed his anger and cruelty upon the baby boys of Bethlehem, slaying them all in a general massacre of newborns and thereby sending them to eternal glory.

FEAST OF THE HOLY FAMILY

FIRST SUNDAY
AFTER CHRISTMAS

John Chrysostom, *Homilies on the Gospel of Matthew*, 8, 2ff.

St. Joseph, a righteous man of faith, knew full well that Christmas was something shocking: it was for him, and it should also be for us. He was not born with a halo and neither were we; however, behind every responsibility and duty, his life guarded something beautiful that he was called to look after. He listened, trusted, and acted. This beauty helped him conquer every fear and doubt, totally abandoning himself to God's plan. And what about us? We are called to make our families an open and welcoming place for life, a context for self-giving and witnessing, and an environment for sharing and communion.

Continue to marvel at this miraculous event! Palestine persecuted Jesus Christ, and Egypt welcomed him and saved him from his persecutors. . . . The angel thus appeared not to Mary, but to Joseph, and said to him, "Rise, take the child and his mother" (Mt 2:13). He no longer said "take your wife," but "take his mother," for by now Joseph harbored no more doubts and firmly believed in the truth of the mystery. The angel thus spoke to him with greater freedom, not calling Jesus "his son" and Mary "his wife," but telling him to "take the child and his mother, [and] flee to Egypt" (Mt 2:13). He explains the reason for the flight by adding that "Herod is going to search for the child to destroy him" (Mt 2:13). Upon hearing these words, Joseph was not adversely shocked. Despite the fact that the same angel had told him shortly before that the child would save his people, and that it now seemed he could not even save himself, he did not tell the angel that this flight seemed puzzling. Were not that flight, that journey, and that long emigration in contradiction with the promise made earlier by the very same angel? Yet Joseph said nothing of all this, for he was a man of faith.

Ambrose, *Commentary on the Gospel of St. Luke*, 2, 58-60

"Now, Master, you may let your servant go / in peace, according to your word, / for my eyes have seen your salvation, / which you prepared in sight of all the peoples, / a light for revelation to the Gentiles, / and glory for your people Israel" (Lk 2:29-32). These are precisely the words of Simeon that the Liturgy of the Hours presents in the compline prayers to accompany our nightly repose. What is our peace? What is our repose? We must put all our hope in Christ and become his witnesses regardless of our age, social status, occupation, or cultural background.

"Now there was a man in Jerusalem whose name was Simeon. This man was righteous and devout, awaiting the consolation of Israel" (Lk 2:25). The birth of the Lord was witnessed not only by angels, prophets, shepherds, and his parents, but also by elderly and righteous men. All ages, both sexes, and the miraculous events themselves give witness: a virgin gives birth, a barren woman has a son, a mute man speaks, Elizabeth prophesies, the Wise Men worship, the child in his mother's womb leaps with joy, a widow gives thanks, and a righteous man awaits. . . . See what an extraordinary abundance of grace is outpoured to all upon the birth of the Lord! And as foretold, it is denied to the unbelievers but not to the righteous. So it is that Simeon prophesies that the Lord Jesus Christ has come for both the ruin and the resurrection of many, to distinguish between the righteous and the unrighteous according to their merits, and to give us—as the true and just Judge—punishment and reward according to our deeds.

Solemnity of Mary, Mother of God

January 1

John Damascene, *An Exposition of the Orthodox Faith*, 3, 12

"We might ask: why exactly did God choose from among all women Mary of Nazareth? The answer is hidden in the unfathomable mystery of the divine will. There is one reason, however, which is highlighted in the Gospel: her humility. Dante Alighieri clearly emphasizes this in the last Hymn of Paradise: 'Virgin Mother, daughter of your Son, / lowly and exalted more than any creature, / the fixed goal of eternal counsel' (Paradise, XXXIII, 1-3). . . . Yes, God was attracted by the humility of Mary, who found favor in his eyes (cf. Lk 1:30). She thus became the Mother of God, the image and model of the Church, chosen among the peoples to receive the Lord's blessing and communicate it to the entire human family. This 'blessing' is none other than Jesus Christ" (Pope Benedict XVI, Angelus, December 8, 2006, *www.vatican.va*).

We proclaim, in an absolute sense, that the Blessed Virgin is truly and properly the Mother of God. Indeed, just as he who was born of her is God, so by consequence is she who generated the true God—who took flesh through her—the Mother of God. We say that God was born of her without a doubt, but not because the divine Word took his principle of being from her; rather, because that same Word, generated before the very beginning of all time and existing together with the Father and the Holy Spirit forever, contained himself in her womb for our salvation, taking on our human nature through her and becoming generated without changing his own [divine] nature. Indeed, the Blessed Virgin did not simply generate a man, but the true God. . . . So it is that we rightly and truly call Mary the Blessed Mother of God. This title captures indeed the entire mystery of the Incarnation.

Cyril of Alexandria, *Sermons*, 4, 1183

The Church Fathers share their way of talking about Mary, the Mother of God, in a sublime language that makes us feel at the same time like she is right next to us. They are all very poetic when speaking of her, yet it is a poetry that draws us to her side as though we had her close by. Their words seem to come from heaven as we barely stammer with our own, for only the language of the angels can clearly describe our Lady.

Hail, Mother of God, Mary, venerable treasure of the whole world, inextinguishable lamp, crown of virginity, scepter of sound doctrine, indissoluble temple, house of him who cannot be contained in any house, mother and virgin for whom he who comes in the name of the Lord is called blessed in the Gospel; hail, you who welcomed into your blessed and virgin womb him who is immense and uncontainable. The Blessed Trinity is glorified and worshiped because of you, the precious Cross is celebrated and adored throughout the world because of you, heaven exults because of you, the angels and archangels are gladdened because of you, demons are put to flight because of you, the Devil and Tempter has fallen from heaven because of you, and the fallen creature has been lifted to heaven because of you. . . . The only begotten Son of God shines brightly for those who were in darkness because of you, the prophets spoke because of you, the dead rise because of you, the Apostles proclaimed salvation because of you, kings reign in the name of the Blessed Trinity because of you. And who could ever adequately extol this Mary, so worthy of praise? She is both mother and virgin: how marvelous! This miracle overwhelms us with awe.

Athanasius, *On the Incarnation*, 8

The Incarnation of Christ is a one-sided exchange that benefits only humankind. Today we benefit on earth, tomorrow in heaven. So great is his divine generosity that it considers nothing but the good of his favored creatures. Mary's motherhood is an extraordinary gift that makes us both children and heirs. On this day in which we also celebrate the World Day of Peace, let us become people and builders of peace through our actions, first in our families and then throughout the world.

The Son of God truly became the Son of Man so that the sons of man, in other words, of Adam, might become sons of God. Indeed, the Word who was ineffably, inexplicably, and incomprehensibly generated outside of time by the Father comes below to earth, generated in time by Mary, Virgin and Mother, so that those who were first generated below might then become generated above, in other words, in the presence of God. . . . This is the reason he calls himself the Son of Man: so that men might call God their heavenly Father. "Our Father," he says, "in heaven" (Mt 6:9). Therefore, just as we servants of God are of God, so the Lord of the servants has become a mortal son of his own servant, in other words, of Adam, so that the children of Adam, who were mortal, might become children of God. For indeed, as it has been written, "To those who did accept him he gave power to become children of God" (Jn 1:12). The Son of God thus experiences death, insofar as he is generated in the flesh, so that the children of man might participate in the life of God as their Father through the Spirit. He is thus the Son of God by nature; we are instead his children through grace.

Solemnity of the Epiphany

January 6

Leo the Great, *Sermon 32, 1*

"The road is long, / we follow a star. / Slow steps and intrepid hearts / gazing with surety upon the Invisible. / We move toward the Event for its contemplation. / Three men, a star, a child, / and overwhelming joy. / Prostrate, we adore." This poem was written during a pilgrimage to the Holy Land, specifically during worship near the star marking the birthplace of Christ in Bethlehem. Today, Christ reveals himself to us in our hearts and showers us with gifts. What can we give to him?

Therefore, dearest brothers, we recognize the firstfruits of our vocation and our faith in the adoration of the Wise Men. With our souls overflowing with joy, let us celebrate the beginning of our blessed hope. Now, indeed, we have begun to enter into possession of our eternal inheritance; and here it is that the secrets of the Scriptures speaking of Christ have been unlocked for us, and the truth—rejected by the Jews who had become blinded—has been spread to all peoples by his light. Let us therefore venerate the most blessed day in which the author of our salvation became manifest and adore the Omnipotent One in the heavens whom the Wise Men adored as a newborn in the cradle. And as the Wise Men offered him gifts from their treasure chests that were mystical symbols, let us too draw forth gifts worthy of God from within our hearts. He is without a doubt the giver of all good, yet he desires the fruits of our labors: indeed, the Kingdom of Heaven is given not to the one who sleeps, but to those who suffer and keep guard in following the commandments of God.

Ephrem the Syrian, *Commentaries on the Diatessaron*, II, 5, 18-25

The Church Father Ephrem the Syrian wrote a work analyzing Tatian's Diatessaron (written in the second century). It is a single text seeking to unify the narratives of the four canonical Gospels. Here Ephrem focuses on the gifts of the Wise Men, discussing the symbolic and Christological meanings of gold, frankincense, and myrrh.

The star appeared because the prophets had disappeared. The star hastened to explain who he was: the one whom the prophets had so accurately described. . . . The Wise Men, who were passionate star observers, would never have decided to follow the light if the star had not attracted them with its brilliance. The same star drew their love, which had been bound to an ephemeral light, toward the light that never fades. "And they opened their treasure chests and offered him gifts: gold for his human nature, myrrh as a symbol of his death, and frankincense for his divine nature." In other words, gold for a king, frankincense for God, and myrrh for a body to be embalmed; or better yet, gold that he might be praised as one praises his master, and myrrh and frankincense to represent the physician who would heal the wound inflicted by Adam.

Hilary of Poitiers, *Commentary on Matthew*, 1, 5

The hearts of the Wise Men yearn for something grand. In seeing the star, they are attracted not by intellectual questions, but by a light that sheds its rays on their true inner needs. They go on their long journey not for scientific reasons, but rather for reasons that only the heart knows. There is a new light in the sky, different from all the others, pointing to a Child who is a king unlike any other. It is a mystery that has been revealed to the world!

The appearance of a star, which the Wise Men understood right from the beginning, evokes the idea that pagans should come to believe in Christ without delay, and that men who have pulled themselves away from knowledge of God because of scientific convictions should not hesitate to recognize the light that immediately appeared upon his birth. The offering of the gifts effectively expresses Christ's being with all of its meaning, recognizing the king with gold, God with frankincense, and the man with myrrh. And the understanding of the mystery as a whole becomes fully clear through the veneration by the Wise Men: death in the man, resurrection in God, and the power of judgment in the king. Then, by the fact that they are warned against retracing their steps and returning to Herod in Judea, the idea emerges that we are not free to draw our knowledge and understanding from Judea;

rather, we are invited to abandon the path of our old life and to place all our hope and salvation in Christ.

Feast of the Baptism of the Lord

Sunday After January 6

Gregory of Nazianzus, *Oration 39: On the Holy Lights*, 14-16

We celebrate the Baptism of the Lord on the Sunday after the Solemnity of the Epiphany. In his angelus message on January 11, 2009, Pope Benedict XVI said the following: "This was the first act of his public life, recounted in all four Gospels. Having reached the age of about thirty, Jesus left Nazareth, went to the River Jordan and, in the midst of a great crowd of people, had himself baptized by John. Mark the Evangelist writes: 'And when he came up out of the water, immediately he saw the heavens opened and the Spirit descending upon him like a dove; and a voice came down from heaven, "You are my beloved Son; in you I am well pleased"' (Mk 1:10-11). These words 'You are my beloved Son' reveal what eternal life is: it is the filial relationship with God, just as Jesus lived it and as he revealed and gave it to us."

A s John is baptizing others, Jesus approaches. Perhaps, in truth, it is in order to purify the one who baptizes him; without a doubt, however, it is to bury the old Adam in the waters, sanctifying the Jordan before all of them, or, more precisely, for all of them, so that they who were body and soul might begin to live through water and the Spirit. The Baptist does not allow it, but Jesus is determined. "I need to be baptized by you" (Mt 3:14), says the lamp to the Sun, the voice to the Word, the friend to the Bridegroom, the greatest among those born of women (see Mt 11:11; Lk 7:28) and of all creatures to the Firstborn Son, he who leapt in his mother's womb to him who was praised in the womb; the precursor and forerunner to him who had come and will come again. "I need to be baptized by you." He could have added to this, "And for you." Indeed, he was sure he would be baptized with martyrdom.

Chromatius of Aquileia, *Sermon 34*, 1-3

Celebration is one of the aspects of our life, and it will become even more so in heaven. We celebrate so many different anniversaries, but so few people remember to celebrate the day of their Baptism; in fact, very few even know when they were baptized. It would be good to renew our remembrance of such an important moment in our life, and it would be helpful if we made it meaningful in our families and communities. Dear reader, on what day were you and I baptized?

Oh, what an immense mystery is in this heavenly Baptism! The Father makes himself heard from heaven, the Son has appeared on earth, and the Holy Spirit reveals himself in the form of a dove. In reality we cannot speak of a true Baptism or a true remission of sins where the truth of the Trinity is missing, nor can the remission of sins be granted without belief in the perfect Trinity. The one, true Baptism is that of the Church, and it happens only once: we are immersed in it one time only, and we come out purified and renewed. We are purified because we become cleansed of the filth of sins, and we are renewed because we rise to a new life after having laid down the decrepitude of sin. This bath of Baptism makes man whiter than snow, not in the color of his skin, but in the splendor of his spirit and the candor of his soul. So it is that the heavens opened at the Baptism of the Lord, showing that this bath of regeneration opens wide the doors to the Kingdom of Heaven in accordance with the words of the Lord: "No one can enter the kingdom of God without being born of water and Spirit" (Jn 3:5). Thus, one who is reborn and who does not neglect to preserve the grace of his Baptism will enter; on the contrary, one who is not reborn will not enter.

CHRISTMAS TIME

Leo the Great, *Sermon 31*, 1ff.

There is a story of a fourth Wise Man who came late, having given the gifts he had brought for Jesus to those in need along his way. He therefore arrived empty-handed and embarrassed because he had nothing to offer. He held out his empty hands, and to his great surprise Mary gave him the little Child Jesus to hold in his arms. This is just a tale, not the Gospel, but I still think that the real Wise Men must have had a similar experience in the depths of their souls. In other words, moving beyond the gifts that they brought, they must have experienced the powerful feeling of having received an extraordinary gift: seeing God in a child and the Child who was God.

The three men (the Wise Men) allow themselves to be led by the light from the heavens, fix their eyes upon the glimmer of the star that precedes and guides them, and contemplate it without ever growing weary. Thus, they who considered it a duty in good sense to seek out the birth of a king that had been revealed to them by a sign were led to the knowledge of truth by the splendor of grace. Yet he who took on the condition of a servant, and came not to judge but to be judged, chose Bethlehem for his birth and Jerusalem for his Passion. The desire of the Wise Men is thus fulfilled: they are led by the star to the Child, the Lord Jesus Christ.

John Chrysostom, *Homilies on the Gospel of John*, 11, 1-2

As was always the case in the pagan world, the encounter between the divine and the human is not one of equals. It is not an encounter of equals for Christianity either, but the shocking thing is that it works solely to the advantage of humankind. During Advent and Christmas, we often hear the phrase "God became like us to make us like him": this is because he holds back nothing and yet loses nothing of himself out of love for us.

"And the Word became flesh / and made his dwelling among us" (Jn 1:14). After having stated that those who accept him are children of God and born of God, he points to the reason for this indescribable honor. . . . He became the Son of Man, despite being the Son of God, in order to turn all men into sons of God. A sublime being entering into a relationship with such a lowly being does no harm to his own reputation, yet raises that other being up from its lowness: this is precisely what was fulfilled in Christ. He did not diminish his divine nature in any way by this lowering of himself, yet we who had been living in darkness and disgrace were raised up to ineffable glory. . . . He lives forever now in this dwelling; he has taken up our flesh not in order to leave it behind after a short while, but to keep it with him for all eternity.

Gregory of Nyssa, *The Great Catechism*, 15, 2-3

God always listens to our prayers and sees our weaknesses. He knows that we are inclined toward sin, but he loves us all the more because of this. God is love, and "no one has greater love than . . . to lay down one's life for one's friends" (Jn 15:13). Jesus did just that for us on the Cross, but he had already shown us his mercy with his birth by "taking the form of a slave" (Phil 2:7) in order to set us free.

D o you want to know the reason God was born among men? If you exclude the beneficent works of God from your life, you will be unable to say which aspects of it allow you to recognize divinity. For the benefits we receive allow us to know the Benefactor: by considering what happens around us, we are able to imagine the nature of the Benefactor through analogy. Thus, if love of humanity is a characteristic proper to the divine nature, there you have the reason you sought: the reason for the presence of God among humanity. Our worn-out nature needed a physician; fallen man needed someone to lift him back up; he who had lost his life needed the Author of life . . . the slave sought a liberator, the prisoner sought a defender, and man held under the yoke of slavery sought a redeemer. And were these reasons so small and insignificant that God might hesitate to come down to us and heal our human nature, which lay in such a wretched and unhappy condition?

Leo the Great, *Sermon 31*, 1ff.

There is no private and exclusive guest list for entering into heaven, but there is certainly a festive garment to be worn: it must be put together throughout our earthly existence. We should not push or skip the line in order to get in, however, because the Lord has shown the path not just to us, but to all men and women of good will. A star, a light, an encounter, or an event can change our lives if we are willing to set out on the journey.

In reality, despite having chosen the Israelite nation and a given family within this nation from which to take on our shared human nature, he nonetheless did not wish to hide the firstfruits of his coming within the restricted confines of his birth home. On the contrary, he who deigned to be born for all wished to immediately present himself to all. So a star of unusual radiance appeared to three Wise Men of the East, the most brilliant and beautiful of all stars, which easily attracted the eyes and hearts of the men who contemplated it. In this way, it could be understood that this unusual sight granted them was not entirely gratuitous. He who granted this sign to those observers of the skies also granted them the corresponding understanding; what he brought them to understand he also brought them to seek; and once they sought, he let himself be found.

Augustine, *The Confessions*, 4, 12, 18-19

"Go ahead and move from continent to continent, kingdom to kingdom, riches to riches, or pleasure to pleasure: you will not find the happiness you seek. The world and all it contains cannot fulfill the immortal soul any more than a pinch of flour can satisfy the hunger of a starving man." May these words of the Holy Curé of Ars serve as a reminder when reflecting on the birth of Christ, who chose to be poor and lowly. What we really seek—true happiness—is found in feeling oneself to be freely loved; and in being loved, being chosen; and in being chosen, being sent.

What profit do you gain from your long and incessant traveling down bitter and painful paths? There is no tranquility where you seek it. You seek what you seek, but it is not where you seek it. You seek a happy life in a land of the dying (see Ps 27:8-13): it is not there. How could a life be happy where life is missing? Our life, our true Life, descended into the world, took our death upon his back and destroyed it with the superabundance of his life; he called out to us in a thundering voice to come back from the world to him, to the sanctuary whence he first came to us by entering the sacrarium of a virgin, where his human creation—our mortal flesh—was united to him as though a bride, that it might not remain mortal forever; then from there, he came forth "like a bridegroom from his chamber, / and like an athlete joyfully . . . [running his] course" (Ps 19:6), making himself known without delay through word and deed, death and life, descent and ascent, making himself known that we might return to him. And he departed from before our eyes that we might return to our hearts, where we find him. Indeed he left; yet behold, he is here.

Leo the Great, *Sermon 21*, 2-3

We have often heard the expression "you don't know who you're dealing with," delivered in a haughty or domineering tone. We should learn how to reinterpret it, directing it at ourselves and our own nature as God's creatures. It should be not for imposing ourselves upon others, but for recognizing ourselves as God's children. If only we realized whose heirs we all are!

I t was suitable for the Christ, the power and wisdom of God (see 1 Cor 1:24), to be born as he was: conformed to us in his humanity and superior to us in his divinity. Indeed, if he had not been true God, he would not have brought the remedy; and if he had not been true man, he could not have been our model. So it was that upon the birth of the Lord the exultant angels sang, "Glory to God in the highest," and announced, "On earth peace to those on whom his favor rests" (Lk 2:14). They could see the heavenly Jerusalem forming from all the nations of the world. If the angels in all their magnanimity so rejoiced in this inerrable work of divine goodness, should not men in their lowliness be glad and delight in it? Thus, let us give thanks to God the Father through his Son in the Holy Spirit. . . . O Christian, be conscious of your dignity, and having been made to participate in the divine nature, do not return to your previous baseness by behaviors unworthy of your descent. Remember who your head is and of whose body you are a part.

Fulgentius of Ruspe, *Sermons for the Feast of St. Stephen*, 1, 3-6

God's providential "imagination" brings St. Stephen and St. Paul together at a moment in which they embody opposing positions on the human and religious levels. Yet this incompatibility, even sealed by Paul's consent to Stephen's martyrdom, is transformed through the martyr's forgiveness and the action of the Holy Spirit into an encounter that begins to change the life of the future Apostle to the Gentiles. Those who look with the eyes of love overcome hatred and death!

Thus driven by love of Christ, we exhort good men to persevere in goodness and seek to draw wicked men away from evil. . . . And may those who are good remain good unto the end; and may those who are wicked instead pull themselves as far away from their wickedness as possible. And may the hope for justice not make the good man negligent nor the awareness of his iniquity make the wicked man despair; rather, may the former keep himself rooted firmly in goodness and the latter promptly reject evil. May the good man fear falling and the wicked man strive to redeem himself. Therefore, let anyone who is wicked lie prostrate with Paul in his wickedness, that he may be raised up to goodness with him; indeed, he too fell down as a wicked man to then raise himself up as a good man. He was knocked down as a wicked man and lifted himself back up as a just man; he fell as a cruel persecutor and got up as a proclaimer of truth. Falling as an impious man he lost the light of the eyes, but then getting up as a just man he received the light of the heart. And he thereby united with Stephen; once a wolf, he became a lamb. . . . They both deserve to inherit the Kingdom of Heaven because of charity: this, therefore, is the source and origin of all goodness, the glorious bulwark, and the path that leads to heaven. Those who walk in charity cannot err and need not fear. It guides us, protects us, and leads us to our final destination.

Gregory of Nazianzus, *Oration 29*, 19-20

Salvation history, our entire existence, and the search for true happiness are all summed up in Christ for those who have faith (see Eph 1:3-10). The birth and infancy narratives are not fables or fairy tales; they are the fulfillment of the prophecies of the Old Testament and therefore of God's promise of love for humanity. This was revealed by the Father and the Holy Spirit in the Baptism of Jesus and on the Mount of Transfiguration.

e was carried in the womb of his mother in the true sense, and was truly recognized by the prophet, who exulted while yet in the womb before the Word by whom he was conceived. He was wrapped in swaddling clothes, and coming back to life he threw off the bands of burial cloth. It is true that he was laid in a manger, but then he was celebrated by the angels, marked by the star, and adored by the Wise Men. Why do you marvel at what is seen by the eyes, while you do not observe what the mind and heart can perceive? He was forced to flee into Egypt, but he put to flight the errant ways of the Egyptians. He received no visibility or human honors from the Jews; but according to David his face was more handsome than that of all the children of men, and on the mount, in the manner of lightning, it would shine and become brighter than the sun so as to foreshadow his future splendor. He was baptized as a man, it is true, but he took sins onto himself as God; he was not baptized because he needed to be purified, but so that he might bring sanctity to the waters themselves.

Leo the Great, *Sermon 21, 2*

Let us admire the beautiful hymn that St. Paul includes in his Letter to the Philippians, in which Jesus is described as both truly human as well as our Redeemer: "Though he was in the form of God, / [he] did not regard equality with God something to be grasped. / Rather, he emptied himself, / taking the form of a slave, / coming in human likeness; / and found human in appearance, / he humbled himself, / becoming obedient to death, / even death on a cross. / Because of this, God greatly exalted him / and bestowed on him the name / that is above every name, / that at the name of Jesus / every knee should bend, / of those in heaven and on earth and under the earth, / and every tongue confess that / Jesus Christ is Lord, / to the glory of God the Father" (Phil 2:6-11).

A nd so it was that the Word of God, God himself, the Son of God, who was in the beginning with God, and through whom all things were made and without whom nothing was made, became man to free man from eternal death. He lowered himself to take on our lowly nature without diminishing his majesty; remaining what he was, he took on what he was not; he united the form of a slave to the form in which he was one with God the Father. . . . His majesty became adorned with lowliness, his strength with weakness, his eternity with mortality. . . . The true God and true man were united in the person of the Lord Jesus so that, in accordance with the requirements of our salvation, a onc and only mediator between God and man might die by one part of himself and rise by the other.

Gregory the Great, *Homilies*, 1, 8

We always remember a special encounter, and a meaningful event can affect our future. When it is Christ whom we encounter, in joy and suffering, it is always an event that changes our life, guiding it toward heaven and happiness. The shepherds could certainly have hoped for anything that night in Bethlehem, but it was attributable to the providential design of God alone that they were at the center of the most often told story in the world and that this filled their souls with exuberance. There is nothing left to do but sing the Gloria together with the angels!

He was before the beginning of time in his divine nature, and came into our nature during an era of history. Thus, if he who is eternal has become our companion in time, we can say that he has come into a realm that is foreign to him. And since the prophet says that every man is like straw, when the Lord became man he changed our straw into grain, for he says of himself: "Unless a grain of wheat falls to the ground and dies, it remains just a grain of wheat" (Jn 12:24). This is also the reason he is placed in the manger upon his birth, so that he might feed all of the faithful, represented by the animals, with the wheat of his flesh. And what does the appearance of the angel to the shepherds who were keeping watch and the light that surrounded them mean, if not that the ones who lovingly keep guard over the flock of the faithful have the privilege of seeing more heavenly things than others? Divine grace pours abundantly over them while they piously watch over the flock. The angel announces that the King has been born, and the choirs of angels echo and sing, "Glory to God in the highest / and on earth peace to those on whom his favor rests" (Lk 2:14).

Gregory of Nazianzus, *Oration 38, 1*

Gregory of Nazianzus urges us to look at the Christmas celebration with a new spirit that overcomes materialism and consumerism. We want to celebrate without forgetting who the true guest of honor is. It is Jesus Christ, yet we too are honored guests with him precisely in virtue of his birth. This does not mean setting aside traditions and ornaments; rather, it means being aware that these are simply accessories to the true and proper celebration of this special time in the liturgical year.

I too, will proclaim the intensity and power of this day: he who was not generated from the flesh has become , flesh, the Word has taken shape, the invisible has become visible, the intangible has become tangible, he who is timeless has come to exist within time, the Son of God has become the Son of Man, and "Jesus Christ is the same yesterday, today, and forever" (Heb 13:8)! The feast that we are celebrating is God coming down among men so that we might go up to God, or (to state it better) return to God so that, having abandoned the old man, we might put on the new man. And just as we died in the old Adam, so we live in Christ; indeed, we are born, put on the cross, buried, and risen with Christ. Thus let us celebrate divinely and not as they often do during public celebrations: not with a worldly spirit, but rather an otherworldly one; not celebrating what is ours, but rather he who is ours or, to state it better, he who is the Lord; not celebrating what causes infirmity, but rather what heals; not what regards creation, but rather regeneration.

John Chrysostom, *Homilies on the Gospel of Matthew*, 8, 2ff.

Following Christ is demanding and requires certain trials. The Scriptures are filled with such examples of fidelity and obedience. The lives of the saints also recount challenging episodes full of suffering and misunderstandings sometimes even caused by people in the Church; yet "the one who perseveres to the end will be saved" (Mt 24:13). In fact, trials are followed by rewards. We should always keep a crucifix with us, and when we are tired, discouraged, or overwhelmed, let us look to him who was "obedient to death, / even death on a cross" (Phil 2:8).

We should expect temptations and dangers right from the very first days of our life. Indeed, consider the fact that this happened immediately to Jesus, right from the moment he was in his crib. He had only just been born, and already the rage of a tyrant was unleashed against him, forcing him to seek refuge in a land of exile, and his pure and innocent mother was forced to flee with him to a foreign land. This way in which God works shows you that when you have the honor of being committed to some ministry or spiritual service and you find yourselves surrounded by infinite dangers and forced to endure cruel tragedies, you need not be concerned or say to yourself, "Why am I, who expected a crown, praises, glory, and ample compensation for having carried out the will of God, being so poorly treated?" May this example thus give you the strength to firmly bear misfortunes and help you understand that the usual fate of spiritual men is this: to have trials and tribulations as inseparable companions.

Leo the Great, *Letter 28, 2*

God's plans are not our plans. This should only uplift us and give us peace! We often think we can organize everything, planning as though we were eternal. Christmas tells us how God enters into our history: he knocks on the door of our heart, neither forcing it nor knocking it down. The door of the heart opens from the inside.

This only eternal Son of an eternal Father was born of the Holy Spirit and the Virgin Mary. This temporal birth neither adds anything to nor takes anything away from his divine and eternal birth; yet it served wholly for the redemption of man, who had been deceived. Through its power it was to conquer death and weaken the Devil, who had control over death up until that point. We could not have conquered sin or the author of death if he— who could not be contaminated by sin or kept prisoner by death—had not taken on our nature and made it his own. . . . "For a child is born to us, a son is given us; / upon his shoulder dominion rests. / They name him Wonder-Counselor, God-Hero, Father-Forever, Prince of Peace" (Is 9:5).

Rufinus of Aquileia, *Commentary on the Apostles' Creed*, 8-9

"By sending us the Holy Spirit, the good Lord acted toward us like a great king who gives his minister the charge of guiding one of his followers by telling him, 'You will accompany this man everywhere, and lead him safely back to me.' How wonderful it is to be accompanied by the Holy Spirit! He is an excellent guide. And to think that there are some people who would rather hear nothing of following him." Through these words of the Holy Curé of Ars, we can recognize the creative, renewing, and unifying presence of the Trinity during Christmas time.

It is already here that she begins to understand the majesty of the Holy Spirit. Indeed, regarding this point, the words of the Gospel affirm that when the angel spoke to the Virgin and told her, "Behold, you will conceive in your womb and bear a son, and you shall name him Jesus" (Lk 1:31), and she replied, "How can this be, since I have no relations with a man?" (Lk 1:34), the angel of God then explained, "The holy Spirit will come upon you, and the power of the Most High will overshadow you. Therefore the child to be born will be called holy, the Son of God" (Lk 1:35). Thus, observe how the Trinity cooperates interchangeably. . . . And although only the Son is born of the Virgin, the Most High and the Holy Spirit are also present so that the virgin conception and birth might be sanctified.

Acknowledgments

Permission to use other passages cited in this book was graciously provided by the publishers, to whom we express our thanks. Excerpts were translated directly from the Italian edition of this book:

Bosio, G., E. Dal Covolo, and M. Maritano. *Introduzione ai Padri della Chiesa: Secoli III e IV* [Introduction to the Church Fathers: Third and Fourth Centuries]. Turin, Italy: SEI, 1993.

Bosio, G., E. Dal Covolo, and M. Maritano. *Introduzione ai Padri della Chiesa—Secoli IV e V* [Introduction to the Church Fathers: Fourth and Fifth Centuries]. Turin, Italy: SEI, 1995.

Starowieyski, M. (ed.). *I Padri vivi—Anno A* [The Living Fathers—Year A]. Rome, Italy: Città Nuova, 1980.

Starowieyski, M. (ed.). *I Padri vivi—Anno B* [The Living Fathers—Year B]. Rome, Italy: Città Nuova, 1984.

Starowieyski, M., and J. Miazek (eds.). *I Padri vivi* [The Living Fathers]. Rome, Italy: Città Nuova, 1982.

La teologia dei padri: Volume 2 [The Theology of the Fathers: Volume 2]. Rome, Italy: Città Nuova, 1974.

La teologia dei padri: Volume 3 [The Theology of the Fathers: Volume 3]. Rome, Italy: Città Nuova, 1975.

About the Author

Marco Pappalardo is a Salesian Cooperator, a past member of the National Council for Youth Pastoral Care of the Italian Bishops' Conference, and a member of the diocesan office for social communications of the Archdiocese of Catania, in Italy. He is a freelance journalist and author of several books in Italian. He is a literature teacher at Don Bosco High School in Catania.

INDEX OF
CHURCH FATHERS